Uh Hello…
I'm Over Here!

How to become more confident
and visible in midlife

Rebecca Perkins

The author greatly appreciates you taking the time to read her work. Please consider leaving a review where you bought the book, or telling your friends about it to help spread the word.

You can sign up to Rebecca's mailing list at http://rebperkins.com/monday-morning-signup/, and receive her Monday Morning Food for Thought emails, a great way to start the week. You'll also be the first to know of what she's publishing next.

Cover design: Samantha Redfern
Formatting: Polgarus Studio

for my friend and mentor Tess Marshall

Acknowledgments

For those friends who have read **Uh Hello.....I'm Over Here!** and worked through the questions, your support has been invaluable. Thank you. Book writing, although a solitary occupation, is never done in isolation; it is always a joint effort and I could not have done it without the love and encouragement of my tribe.

Thank you all. You are my rocks! You show me how to be the best version of myself.

Thank you to my editor Carol Pearson for being just as excited about this book as I am. Thank you for your cheerleading and your insight!

Contents

Uh Hello, I'm Over Here!

Hello my lovely midlife friend

I decided to write this book after countless conversations with friends and reading so much negativity in the press about midlife. It saddens me to be continually reading about women in midlife who feel that they have become **invisible**. They say they walk into a room and nobody notices them. I hear so many stories of lack of confidence and low self-esteem, of women telling me they feel they no longer have any value to the world.

This makes my heart break. I so long for us to feel valued, confident, respected, in our groove, alive and vibrant once again. I feel like this because I am in many respects still one of those women. There are days when I do feel a lack of confidence and wonder if it is because of my age. I can't help but compare myself with younger women who are achieving great things in their life and wonder if it's too late for me to really make a difference. And because you have this book, I'm guessing that you may very well feel the same way. Or at least you are feeling that something has to change, yet you can't quite put your finger of what that is.

Thank you for purchasing **Uh Hello….I'm Over Here!**
I'm so thrilled, truly. My intention is that it will be all that
you hoped for AND more! I hope this book becomes your
companion through midlife, helping to ask the right
questions of you at just the right time.

So, what's this book **Uh Hello….I'm Over Here!** all
about?

It's a short and powerful four-chapter book, and I like to
think of it as a four-day workshop. It's written for ALL
women in midlife who are looking for a bit of a shake up!

On the surface? It's about taking practical steps that will
guide you out of the shadows to become more visible in
midlife.

But what's it about really? Oh, it's about understanding,
embracing and appreciating who you are now and how
you want to be and live from now on. It's about loving the
woman you are. It's about reconnecting with yourself and
celebrating midlife. It's about appreciating the choices we
have. It's about making those choices. And above all it's
about self-love!

It's designed for all women, and especially those who have
self-doubt, who feel undervalued, and invisible. It's for
women who know there is so much more to life than they
currently feel. It's for those women who are ready to
explore.

My intention is that by the end of the book:

- You will have begun to identify and understand some of your outdated beliefs especially those beliefs that are holding you back from living a more fulfilling second half of your life.
- You will understand yourself a lot more, and that has to be a good thing! It might feel a little scary as you begin asking yourself questions you might never have asked before, but I'm here to guide you along the way.
- You will have begun to take steps towards a future you can be excited about. Hurrah! Imagine that for a moment—to be excited about the future!
- You will feel braver and more courageous because step by step, you will be investing time in exploring what's important to you for your life.
- you will stand taller and you will most certainly have begun to be **VISIBLE!**

Using my experience as a coach, I'll give you lots of practical tips and exercises as well as a ton of questions to ask yourself. Parts of the book are set out like a workbook for you to complete. I'll remind you again later but it might be worth noting on your shopping list that a brand new, gorgeous journal would be a good idea (make it a big one, not a tiny handbag-sized one).

It's been exciting writing this book as I've created

something that I've been working through too! Believe me: I've been answering all the questions I've asked and tasting my own medicine! And please don't worry, my lovely, if you've never done anything like this before because we'll take it step-by-step. You can go at your own pace. In fact, it's probably better to go slowly, giving each chapter time to be fully understood and absorbed.

I really believe that it's time for us to stand up and be noticed for the fabulous women we are. Don't you?

So where do we start?

There is no doubt that midlife is a time of major upheaval for most of us. There are a whole range of changes we are having to deal with both physically and emotionally.

Some mornings I feel like my grandmother getting out of bed! Where did those aching joints come from? My ankles, my legs, padding to the bathroom first thing in the morning can take a little effort! Weight gain affects so many of us, especially as we hit menopause. The fact is it takes a lot more effort to keep fit and I find that frustrating. Menopause can play havoc with our emotions too, can't it? I'm not the only one who cries for no apparent reason, am I? Forgetfulness, hot flushes, skin breakouts are all part of the joys I'm discovering at this perimenopausal phase! No wonder we're finding it difficult to embrace the ageing process at times.

What brings us down often is that at midlife we come up for air for the first time in a long time. We are facing major changes in our lives. Our children have left or are preparing to leave home. We've faced a loved one's illness or a scare of our own. Some of us have gone from married to single—any of these can act as the trigger that awakens us to life around us. We come to realise that life is short and we probably still have unfulfilled dreams. Many of us become aware that we've been living our lives unconsciously.

This realisation can be deeply painful. It often leads us to retreat into our shells further, to hide away and become resentful, bitter, or scared. We really don't want to be living the rest of our life filled with regret and frustration, but some days it seems impossible to put ourselves out there.

These realisations all come from hard learned personal experience and I want to show you how you can look forward to a fulfilling second half of your life.

Most of us have at some time or another felt invisible, ignored and of no value. We lack in confidence, we have low self-esteem. And that's not good, right? We so often overlook our value and our successes, we tend to focus on what's not working rather than what is and what's good in our lives. We find it so easy to focus on our weaknesses in midlife, the things we can no longer do or the things we find difficult. Remaining stuck here can so easily lead to depression and despondency.

What I'm suggesting firstly, is that to find and reconnect with our confidence once again we must focus on what we're good at—our strengths—what we do well and with ease, those things we take for granted or don't give the recognition they deserve. Things like:

- raising a family
- inspiring and motivating others
- caring for others
- being an entrepreneur
- our career success
- being a great friend
- making a difference in others' lives or our community
- being a homemaker

It might be a good idea to share this exercise with a close friend. We don't often see the things we do well and with ease. Ask a friend what your talents are; she might tell you some things that you've taken for granted. Ask her what you do really well. Invite her to list the things that she admires in you. And in turn, offer to do the same for her.

"What would Jane do in this situation?", "Susan always sums things up so succinctly", "Amanda has such a great relationship with her children, what does she do differently?" These are the things I'm talking about.

As women, we have a shocking tendency to compare ourselves to others. I used to do it all the time (it's a little less often these days). For example, I might compare my lack of career success when I was younger with a friend who was very successful…failing to see that I have a great relationship with my children whilst another friend struggles with motherhood. How can that be a fair comparison? Can you see just how crazy that is?

I am grateful that I have come to realise that comparison is a waste of time. It's time to give this up!

Each of us has a different story, a different experience, a different reason for what we do and why we do it. We are the only one on our particular journey. We are unique. Our stories are unique. What works for one woman will not work for another. We are never going to thrive by comparing like for like. Why mimic others? Why try to copy someone else? Save yourself the heartache—really!

So are you ready to begin?

Before we do so, let me give you my suggestion on how to best work through this book. You can then make up your own mind for what's going to work best for you.

First of all get yourself that journal I mentioned earlier in the introduction; you're going to need it (the bigger the better)! Treat yourself to something that you're going to love writing in, so not a refill pad from the local supermarket! Next, read through the first chapter without doing any of the exercises, then put the book down and read no further! When you're able to set aside some time (either in one long session or in a few shorter sessions) begin to work through the questions. Don't be in a rush to work through the book. You will benefit from taking your time. There is no hurry. When you're happy that you've completed the first chapter, then and only then move onto Chapter 2 and once again read it through first before answering the questions. And so on until you've got through all four chapters. You can of course do it in whatever way works for you, but it's been designed to give you time to really think about the questions and dig deep for your answers.

Another option would be to work through each chapter with a friend or couple of friends. Why not set aside several hours in your favourite coffee shop or even a day at the weekend when you can really get into the questions and have fun together? Hmmm, that's got me thinking about creating a workshop! How does that sound?

Okay, let's take a moment before we go any further. Close your eyes, take a few long, slow breaths, and think about where you are in your life right now and what you'd love to be different. Think of just one thing that you'd love to change right now, one thing that would have a positive impact on your wellbeing and happiness. Get a sense of the feelings you want to feel, and how you want to show up in life. Breathe it all in. It may well bring up some strong emotions. That's okay. Let whatever happens happen. Lovingly allow whatever comes to the surface.

Ask yourself this question: "What do I want to be different in how I think and feel about my life by the time I've finished reading and completing the exercises in this book?" Setting an intention is a great way to begin the process of positive change.

Okay— let's begin.

Chapter 1
Invisibility + Life Review

I believe we get to a point in midlife when we are no longer prepared to be defined by those around us. Do you remember Lesson 50 from my book "Best Knickers Always: 50 Lessons for Midlife"? Maya Angelou reminds us,

"Each of us has the right, that possibility, to invent ourselves daily. If a person does not invent herself, she will be invented. So, to be bodacious enough to invent ourselves is wise."

I decided to include one of her poems here as a reminder to ourselves of just how amazing we are. You may well not be feeling that right now but I ask you to suspend all judgment of yourself, all your self-criticism and read the words of the *phenomenal* and bodacious Maya Angelou, the inspiration in so many women's lives. Read them slowly and take them to heart. Imagine filling her shoes, imagine standing tall, imagine being proud of who you are and how far you've come.

Phenomenal Women - Maya Angelou

Pretty women wonder where my secret lies.
I'm not cute or built to suit a fashion model's size
But when I start to tell them,
They think I'm telling lies.
I say,
It's in the reach of my arms,
The span of my hips,
The stride of my step,
The curl of my lips.
I'm a woman
Phenomenally.
Phenomenal woman,
That's me.
I walk into a room
Just as cool as you please,
And to a man,
The fellows stand or
Fall down on their knees.
Then they swarm around me,
A hive of honey bees.
I say,
It's the fire in my eyes,
And the flash of my teeth,
The swing in my waist,
And the joy in my feet.
I'm a woman
Phenomenally.

Phenomenal woman,
That's me.
Men themselves have wondered
What they see in me.
They try so much
But they can't touch
My inner mystery.
When I try to show them,
They say they still can't see.
I say,
It's in the arch of my back,
The sun of my smile,
The ride of my breasts,
The grace of my style.
I'm a woman
Phenomenally.
Phenomenal woman,
That's me.
Now you understand
Just why my head's not bowed.
I don't shout or jump about
Or have to talk real loud.
When you see me passing,
It ought to make you proud.
I say,
It's in the click of my heels,
The bend of my hair,
the palm of my hand,
The need for my care.

'Cause I'm a woman
Phenomenally.
Phenomenal woman,
That's me.

Are you willing to explore this kind of commitment to yourself, this resonant belief of Maya Angelou's? Her belief that she, and we are *Phenomenal Women*?

Are you open to looking at and beginning to appreciate your importance in your *own* eyes?

Are you willing to ask yourself deep and meaningful questions?

Are you prepared to shed your old skin (if that's what's appropriate)?

Are you eager to step into your own power, your own beauty, your own wisdom and grace?

Look at this marvellous quote by Jodie Foster:

"I'm not interested in being perfect when I'm older. I'm interested in having a narrative. It's the narrative that's really the most beautiful thing about women." ~ *Jodie Foster*

Ask yourself what's important in and for your life. *What's your narrative?*

WORKBOOK

Invisibility

What does being invisible really mean to me?

_____

_____

_____

_____

_____

_____

_____

_____

How do I experience invisibility in my life?

_____

_____

_____

_____

_____

_____

_____

_____

What does being invisible feel like? What emotions does it bring up?

_____

_____

_____

_____

_____

_____

_____

_____

Am I really invisible? Am I actually ignored and not noticed?

_____

_____

_____

_____

_____

_____

_____

_____

What is perhaps the underlying issue?

_____

_____

_____

_____

_____

_____

_____

_____

What does this tell me about where I am currently in my life?

_____

_____

_____

_____

_____

_____

_____

_____

Life Review

What would I change if I could change just one thing? How great an impact would that have on my life?

_____

_____

_____

_____

_____

_____

_____

_____

What are my needs and goals for midlife?

_____

_____

_____

_____

_____

_____

_____

What would I say to my younger self today?

_____

_____

_____

_____

_____

_____

_____

_____

How proud would the girl I once was be of the woman I am today?

_____

_____

_____

_____

_____

_____

_____

_____

_____

What did I dream of as a young adult?

_____

_____

_____

_____

_____

_____

_____

_____

_____

How differently do I feel about myself now to 10 years ago/20 years ago/30 years ago?

_____

_____

_____

_____

_____

_____

_____

_____

_____

When was the last time I took a risk?

_____

_____

_____

_____

_____

_____

_____

_____

_____

When was the last time I did something for the very first time?

_____

_____

_____

_____

_____

_____

_____

_____

_____

What frightens me now? What frightened me as a child and a young adult?

_____

_____

_____

_____

_____

_____

_____

_____

_____

Do set aside enough time to answer these questions. There will be some that you'll find hard to answer I'm sure. Be aware of the emotions that are raised in doing so. Be kind and gentle with yourself throughout.

How do you feel right now? What have you begun uncovering about yourself?

Here's an exercise that will improve your life immediately. These tips are simple heartfelt ideas that I've used on many occasions when I've needed to instantly feel better and boost my mood.

Five Tips to Immediately Improve your Life

1. Before you get out of bed (or before you fall asleep) make a list in a notebook of five things you are grateful for in your life today. It might be the birdsong you hear on waking, or the comfortable bed you sleep in. It might be that you can glimpse the sun shining through your curtains. It might be knowing that you are moments away from a cup of tea. Keep this up every day for the duration of these four chapters and notice how your life changes. I promise, it absolutely will!

2. Spend five minutes in mindful meditation. Sit comfortably upright or lie on a blanket on the floor. Gently close your eyes and focus your full attention on your breath. Breathe in fully and feel the sensation of your chest and belly rising. Release your breath slowly and fully feel your chest and belly return to resting. Your mind will wander; this is normal. Simply bring your focus back to your breath without criticising yourself. Continue in this way for five minutes or so. Commit to doing this every day whilst you're reading this book. Make a note of how you get on and see what you notice.

3. Play your very favourite song from your feel good playlist—you do have one don't you?! If not, why not create one? You can see a selection from my playlist at the end of "Best Knickers Always: 50 Lessons for

Midlife". How does music change your mood? Which song and artist do you turn to for inspiration?

4. Choose something from your wardrobe that makes you feel good, something that has positive, happy memories - obviously for me that means *Best Knickers. Always!* Do you have a photograph of yourself feeling fabulous in your favourite dress or pair of jeans? Frame it and keep it somewhere close at hand to remind yourself how gorgeous you are.

5. Make the decision to give someone a truly heartfelt compliment today. It might be the barista at your local coffee shop who makes your coffee just the way you like it. It might be a colleague who always seems to smile easily. It might be your child who did as you asked without making a fuss! See what happens when you compliment them. Begin like this, "I really like it that you…"

How different will your life be in four weeks' time if you commit to doing these five things consistently? Will you do it? Why not keep a note of how you feel every few days. Sometimes when we're feeling a bit down in the dumps or we've had a rubbish day this is the best time to follow these five tips. They help us get a different perspective on how we're feeling. Is it worth a go?

Chapter 2
Taking Responsibility

How did you get on in Chapter 1? Were you able to set aside some time for yourself, real time in solitude to answer the questions and do some thinking? I do hope so. If you've yet to complete all the exercises in the first chapter, including the 'Five Tips to Immediately Improve Your Life' then I'm going to suggest that you complete that before progressing to Chapter 2.

Pacing any change is really important. The last thing I want is for you to get to the end of this book with a feeling of overwhelm because of the amount of 'work' there is to be done. Take it easy, take it slowly and savour spending time with yourself. This is a journey my lovely, not a race.

Remember we looked at setting an intention at the beginning of the last chapter? Let's look at this once more. Take a moment to get yourself comfortable wherever you're sitting. Gently close your eyes and focus on your breathing for a few moments. I want you to feel totally relaxed and comfortable. Ask yourself these questions and gently allow the answers to unfold.

"How do I want to feel as I read this book?"

"What is my intention today?"

So, are you set? Are you ready to start digging around a little more?

In this second chapter, we're going to look at Responsibility - *Self Responsibility.*

"It is time to stop looking outside yourself for the answers to why you haven't created the life and results you want, for it is you who creates the quality of the life you lead and the results you produce. You - no one else! You must assume 100% responsibility for your life. Nothing less will do." ~ Stephen Covey

Those words of Stephen Covey may well sting a little. For some of us they won't be that easy to digest. He's throwing down the gauntlet, isn't he? All the answers are inside us and responsibility for our life lies fully with us. It would be so much easier if we could have that responsibility lie with someone else at times, wouldn't it?

Think of an area in your life where you'd like things to be different. How responsible or in other words, answerable are you in this area of your life? Putting it another way, what can *you* change? On a scale of 1 to 10 mark it. How differently would you behave if you wanted to move up just one point on the scale?

What would I do and how would I behave differently today if I took responsibility?

_____

_____

_____

_____

_____

_____

_____

_____

What are my core beliefs about responsibility? Is it my duty to be responsible for my life or is it someone else's? (*Sounds crazy and rather obvious but you'd be surprised.*)

_____

_____

_____

_____

_____

_____

_____

_____

_____

Taking full responsibility for our lives is taking back control of the reigns. *It's letting go of blame.* By blaming others, we relinquish control for our own life. Is that what you want to do? This is your life, no one else's.

Therefore, the question is, *how responsible am I for my own invisibility?* How complicit am I? What has been my role?

_____

_____

_____

_____

_____

_____

_____

_____

_____

And this leads on to the big question! *What's this really about?* Self-esteem? Self-worth? Self-confidence? Dissatisfaction? Disillusionment?

I ask you to be honest with yourself here, truly honest. What's really going on? Take a moment, breathe and get writing.

_____

_____

_____

_____

_____

_____

_____

_____

_____

I'm guessing that wasn't the easiest thing to write. I'm really glad you did though, because it is the first step in taking responsibility for your own life.

Let's look at *invisibility* again…Imagine a time in the past when you've felt totally invisible. It might have been at work, in a meeting, at a social gathering, walking down the street… Think of it now through the eyes of your *midlife hero*, or through your own eyes as a strong, empowered woman. This might be a big stretch and leap of faith right now but how different would it feel?

Stand tall. Walk as if you are that woman who takes full responsibility for her life. Think of a woman you admire and hold in high esteem. How does she walk? How does she hold herself? What do you imagine are the words she says when she catches sight of herself in the mirror? Does she treat herself well and with respect?

Try this exercise. Sit and have a coffee at a pavement cafe where you will notice a lot of people walking by (or when you are next at a busy railway station, or at the airport or even on the promenade by the seaside). I want you to imagine what it feels like to be those people passing by. Imagine literally walking in their shoes. What do you notice? What must it be like to be that person, to walk that way? What are they thinking? What is their life like? Think of yourself now. What would people say about the way you walk?

Now, look at your life; take a good long look and decide how responsible you have been in your choices - good and not so good. You can make changes starting today. They don't need to be major changes; sometimes the simplest thing can have a profound effect. Accepting responsibility brings us freedom from the past and opens us up to possibility for the future. Remember this, my friend: *there is no room for regret in life. It changes nothing in the past and only steals the joy from today and the future.*

"Incredible change happens in your life when you decide to take control of what you do have power over instead of craving control over what you don't." - *Steve Maraboli*

Invisibility is something you feel. *People notice you if you take notice of and value yourself.* Who is it that says you're invisible? This isn't about others not noticing you, in that it's something out of your control. This is very much within your control. If you value, respect and acknowledge yourself then believe me, others will value, respect, acknowledge and *notice* you.

There is no fairy godmother coming to rescue you, my dear. It is your responsibility to be the director and producer of your own life. I ask that you acknowledge your role in taking responsibility for your life, for your growth, for your journey. No one will do it for you. No one *can* do it for you. We must be our own hero, our own role model. Yes?

Another way of looking at this question is to ask yourself these questions: Who is invisible to me? Do I notice people? Do I engage with people? Am I waiting for people to jump in and notice me or help me?

_____

_____

_____

_____

_____

_____

_____

_____

_____

If you want to be visible then it's time to step out of the shadows!

If you've already got my book "21 Questions: A New Way of Thinking About Your Midlife" now might be a good time to look at and answer those 21 powerful questions again, once you've finished this book.

Chapter 3
Positive Attitude and Confidence

How did you get on in Chapter 2? Make sure you've taken all the time you need to fully answer the questions. It will be worth it, I promise. There is no hurry. The value lies in doing the exercises, not just reading through them.

If you're ready then let's take the next step now, shall we?

Do I hear you saying "It's all well and good stepping out of the shadows but I just don't have the confidence I used to"?

The transition we go through in midlife can have a fundamental and painful impact on our attitude and confidence. It raises many issues for us that can affect us at a deep emotional level. We often experience self-doubt in midlife that is kicked off as our roles begin to change. If we've had children, they are either leaving home or, if they are still in the nest, they at least no doubt need us less than they did. They are beginning to develop their own lives and don't want Mum around so much. Our very sense of self is often tied up with that of our children and the family. If we've not had children, or menopause is creeping ever closer or indeed we're in the full throes of it, we may face issues around our fertility and the end of any realistic hopes of having children. In the workplace, we may have reached what we see as the glass ceiling and have begun to feel vulnerable as younger colleagues are promoted or seem to be more in favour.

"Who am I?", "I don't know who I am anymore", "I don't recognise the woman I see in the mirror" are questions and comments I hear a lot. Our very identity is so often tied up with that of the family unit. We've become used to hearing ourselves being introduced as someone's mother, or wife, or partner, or daughter.

As women, we are so good at focussing on the negative aren't we? All the endings we're facing—lost youth, lost fertility, children leaving the nest, 'if only', menopause, another decade...

But here's the thing. Does lacking in confidence now mean that you'll never do anything risky, or challenging, or even adventurous again?

Dissatisfaction and a lack of confidence can lead us to shut down rather than open up. Take a look at the following questions and be **honest** in asking yourself where you are dissatisfied in your life. I don't usually ask negatively focussed questions but these offer us a starting point for making changes. It's often easier to know and identify what we don't want rather than what we do, or spot what's not working rather than what is.

How is my work life, my career? Am I where I wanted to be at this stage of life?

_____

_____

_____

_____

_____

_____

_____

_____

_____

How are my relationships?

_____

_____

_____

_____

_____

_____

_____

_____

_____

How is my health?

_____

_____

_____

_____

_____

_____

_____

_____

_____

How about my spiritual life?

_____

_____

_____

_____

_____

_____

_____

_____

_____

And what about self-satisfaction?

_____

_____

_____

_____

_____

_____

There's a lot to look at, right? Take it easy, take it slowly. There isn't a race to get the answer today. Think of it more as an exploration and a way of getting a better understanding of who and where you are now.

If you're feeling up to it here are some further questions:

How am I dealing with ageing?

_____

_____

_____

_____

_____

_____

How do I perceive my achievements?

_____

_____

_____

_____

_____

_____

_____

_____

_____

Do I compare myself regularly with others? Do I compare
what I've **not** done with what others have done?

_____

_____

_____

_____

_____

_____

_____

_____

_____

Do I feel inferior to those with long established careers if I've stayed at home to raise the children?

_____

_____

_____

_____

_____

_____

_____

_____

Am I financially dependent on my partner and feel lacking in value? How does that make me feel?

_____

_____

_____

_____

_____

_____

_____

_____

You've answered some pretty heavy questions and I'm really proud of you for having done so. It's not easy, I know that. You've done something that will help you move forward now in your life because you've looked into the past and can now challenge some long held beliefs about yourself and what's possible for you.

Okay so let's flip it back to the positive.

What are you really ridiculously good at?
What is really good in your life?
What is your wildest dream?
What five achievements have made you feel great about yourself?

There is no place for modesty here, my friend! What can you do easily, something you no doubt take for granted? It could be communicating at a senior level, it might be marathon running. It could be Sudoku, it might be baking a soufflé. It could be listening to your children, or solving a problem for a friend. Make a list right now. I want at least 10 things on that list…ask a friend if you're stuck, they'll definitely be able to help you!

Now it's time to begin looking at *confidence and having a positive attitude* and see how having these will affect our perception of invisibility in midlife.

Confidence and a positive attitude is all an inside job! Nobody else can give them to you.

There are many role models from whom we can learn and they are quite the opposite of invisible in midlife. And I'm not just referring to those who are extrovert in life generally. There are plenty of introverts who ooze confidence and positive attitude.

Who are your female role models? Family, friends, acquaintances, colleagues? Ask yourself these questions and it'll help you understand them so that you can learn from them and apply that knowledge in your own life. (You don't need to know them personally to answer these questions—she might be the woman you notice every morning at the railway station.)

What is it that makes her 'attractive'?
How does she stand?
How does she move?
How does she walk?
What does she stand for?
What makes her stand out?
What is different about her?
What questions would you like to ask her to get inside her head?
What does she do that others don't?
How different is her attitude to life?
How would she walk into a room?
How does she behave?
What could she teach you?

Imagine being this woman for a day. Imagine walking in

her shoes, literally. Get inside her head. Imagine how she would respond to difficult questions. How does she behave? Which women have the type of confidence you admire?

There's a lot of sense in having a "fake it 'til you make it" attitude. Little by little is the key though; I'm not suggesting that you leap headlong into something that terrifies you. Simply ask, "What would be a stretch right now?" "What would be a little challenge right now?" "How good will I feel about myself for having risen to the challenge?"

Who is living the life you admire? How would it feel to be living that life? Take care answering this question; it's not about envy or jealousy but rather finding someone who just seems to have it right and learning from them. So answer it in good spirit.

What's your frame of mind like?
What words can you use to support and encourage yourself?
What are the things you can do that will immediately have an impact?
What actions are you prepared to take immediately?

A great way to start is to walk with attitude. Do you make eye contact with people when you're outside or do you hurry on by, walking with your head down? I dare you to do something different next time you're walking through town, or out in the park. Make eye contact, not in a weird staring way but actually "see" others around you. Note in your journal how it felt. What did you notice?

I'd like to end the chapter with this quote.

"Finally I'm coming to the conclusion that my highest ambition is to be what I already am." ~ *Thomas Merton.*

I love this quote and find it so relevant for what we've been working on. Finding ourselves, looking deep inside is, in a way, a coming home. What if we'd simply forgotten who we were all along?

I think it's time to re-acquaint ourselves, don't you?

Chapter 4
How do you Want to Live?

Now that you've begun to take steps out of the shadows by looking at the part you play in being visible, how do you want to live and be from now on? How would you like to live the second half of your life?

By taking full responsibility and accountability for your life, you free yourself up to make decisions that will affect your life. For some, these are going to be tough decisions around work life, relationships, lifestyle. For others it might just be a little tweak here and there — getting fit, eating more healthily, finding a hobby that inspires you.

Try this exercise called Blue Sky Dreaming, one I often do with clients. Let yourself go with it. There are no rules and there is definitely no place for judging yourself in your writing! (I've also recorded it as an audio if you'd prefer once you read it through. Here's the link to the audio recording - http://rebperkins.com/blue-sky-thinking-rp/)

Blue Sky Dreaming: Creating your Dream Life

What dreams of yours are still alive and kicking? Which ones have you consigned to the back burner, or worse still, the bin?

When was the last time you found time for some daydreaming? For some dream creating? It's something I encourage my clients to do regularly. I do it too. It needn't take long. And the results will be magical.

For this exercise you'll need a journal or notebook, an open and curious mind, some uninterrupted time and your favourite writing pens or pencils.

I hope you're ready to press pause and take 20 minutes or so of your precious time for some daydreaming. I know you're probably not used to taking this kind of time for yourself. You may very well be thinking that this is a waste of time or even worse self-indulgent, when there is a heap of laundry waiting for you or emails to be answered or others needing your time…sound familiar?

Allow me to metaphorically hold your hand a moment and guide you to asking yourself some questions that you may well never have asked yourself. Or if you have, perhaps it's been a very long time since you did.

If you don't have time right now then at the very least mark somewhere in your diary when you are able to find 20 minutes of stillness, of quiet, of solitude, where you won't be disturbed, where there will be no distractions and pinging of phones or email notifications. Do you value yourself enough to do this? Simply reading won't make things happen! Action is required!

Find a quiet cafe or sit in the park, or on the beach if you're lucky enough. You will definitely find it easier to allow yourself to daydream if you're away from home or the office.

This is far too important to try and squeeze into a few minutes; you won't benefit from the exercise unless you give it the time.

Are you ready?

Take a moment to get yourself comfortable, sit in such a way that you are most at ease and alert. You might be sitting on the floor or at a table, the choice is yours; your comfort is the most important here. I want you to read through first without doing anything but listening to the words, allowing them to settle into your subconscious. Notice whatever comes up for you. You might find it challenging, you might not. You might find you get a little emotional or you might not. You might find it exciting and energising or you might not. It's different for everyone.

I'd like you to imagine your life five years from now. You are living your ideal life, you are in your element. Everything has come together perfectly. All the worries and concerns you had are in the past. You came through and it's time to celebrate. You are alive and vibrant and calm. You are happy and energised.

I invite you to create a beautiful, richly sensory picture of that ideal life right now in your mind's eye.

Where are you living?

What surrounds you?

What can you see?

What can you hear?

What can you smell and touch and taste?

Who is with you?

What are you doing?

What do you notice about yourself?

What are you feeling?

What are you thinking?

What are you doing for a living?

How do you spend your leisure time?

How different is your life from five years ago?

How is your health?

How have your relationships changed?

What is your outlook on life like?

What have you achieved to get you to this point today?

What have been your successes?

What changes have you made in your life?

What changes have you made in your personal life?

What are you incredibly proud of having achieved?

How is your future looking?

What dreams came true?

Now that you have read these questions, take some time to close your eyes, settle into the stillness and open your mind and your heart to create a beautiful picture of your life.

When you're ready, pick up your pen or pencil and write. Write whatever comes up. Write from your heart. Write from your gut. No judgment, no critique, no reigning yourself in. This is to be free and powerful and wild.

Go for it!

Remember the Jodie Foster quote right at the start of the book? She said of ageing that "it's the narrative that's the most beautiful thing about women."

This is your chance to write your narrative.

We are nearing the end of this book, so here are a few concluding questions:

What have you learned about yourself?
What is your narrative?
Are you satisfied with where your life is now?
What will you do to change it if you're not?

What's stopping you from doing something different?

Let us become the role models we longed for. Let us show our daughters, nieces, granddaughters and other young women just how we are choosing to live the second half of our lives.

What will it mean for your life if you no longer believe you were invisible, that what you have to offer the world has value?

How differently will you act and live your life? What if you begin today?

What next?

Visit http://rebperkins.com/monday-morning-signup/ to sign up for my mailing list. You'll get a Monday Morning Food for Thought email from me as well as links to blogs, videos and details of when you can expect my next book to be available. I promise not to overload your inbox!

If you enjoyed **Uh Hello… I'm Over Here!** and it's helped you in some way then I'd be delighted if you left a review where you bought this book. Positive reviews make authors very happy! Thank you in advance.

As always, I love to engage with my readers. Please do get in touch via email (info@rebperkins.com) and let me know how you got on.

Do you spend time on Twitter? If so, come and find me there. Let's have a conversation about midlife, the highs and lows, the joys and the tears. Or if Facebook's your social media of choice, you can find me there too.

If you enjoyed this book you may also like these…

"Best Knickers Always: 50 Lessons for Midlife"

"40 Words of Wisdom for my 24 Year Old: A Parenting Manifesto"

"21 Questions: A New Way of Thinking About Your Midlife"

My books are available for download worldwide.

Rebecca Perkins is the author of "Best Knickers Always: 50 Lessons for Midlife". and founder of RebPerkins.com. She has appeared on BBC Radio 4's Woman's Hour and BBC Radio London. She regularly writes for the Huffington Post.

She began writing to make sense of her life after the ending of her 20-year marriage. She is passionate about midlife as a time for renewal and for living the second half of life with enthusiasm and vigour.

Rebecca trained as a Neuro-Linguistic Programming (NLP) Master Practitioner and Coach; she works closely with clients, guiding them to make often profound changes to their lives. She is a talented and dedicated midlife coach, a role model for those wishing to make substantial positive changes in their lives.

Rebecca finds energy in inspiring others. Her greatest joys

include supporting and being surrounded by her children and her partner, taking risks, living in London and celebrating life in her 50s.

Come and find Rebecca on the following social media sites and say hello!

Facebook
https://www.facebook.com/BestKnickersAlways

Instagram
http://instagram.com/beabodacious

Pinterest
http://www.pinterest.com/beabodacious/

Twitter
https://twitter.com/rebperkins1

17614749R00038

Printed in Great Britain
by Amazon